HEDGEHOGS TODAY
A YEARBOOK

by Dennis Kelsey-Wood

Photography by: Isabelle Francais, Michael Gilroy, Louise Bauck, Robert Pearcy, Vincent Serbin and H. Axelrod.

yearBOOKS, INC.
Dr. Herbert R. Axelrod
    President
Neal Pronek
    Chief Editor
Marcy Myerovich
    Editor

yearBOOKS are all photo composed, color separated and designed on Scitex equipment in Neptune, N.J. with the following staff:
COMPUTER ART
  Michael L. Secord
      Supervisor
  Kenneth Bontz
  Sherise Buhagiar
  Patti Escabi
  Sandra Taylor Gale
  Pat Marotta
  Joanne Muzyka
  Robert Onyrscuk
  Tom Roberts

Advertising Sales
George Campbell
    Chief
Amy Manning
    Coordinator

©yearBOOKS,Inc.
1 TFH Plaza
Neptune, N.J. 07753
Completely manufactured in Neptune, N.J.

Adventurous, inquisitive, exciting people have given up hamsters, mice and guinea pigs as their favorite pets and have discovered the exotic dwarf African hedgehog, also called the *pygmy hedgehog or white-bellied hedgehog*, just to name a few. Because it is so new it can be found at only the most progressive petshops. There is very little reliable information available regarding the selection, care and breeding of this charming animal.

By far the world's leading specialist is Dennis Kelsey-Wood. As President of the North American Hedgehog Association, Dennis has written and lectured widely on the subject. He may have singlehandedly made hedgehog keeping a new hobby.

What are yearBOOKs?

Because keeping hedgehogs as pets is growing at a rapid pace, information on their selection, care and breeding is vitally needed in the marketplace. Books, the usual way information of this sort is transmitted, can be too slow. Sometimes by the time a book is written and published, the material contained therein is a year or two old...and no new material has been added during that time. Only a book in a magazine form can bring breaking stories and current information. A magazine is streamlined in production, so we have adopted certain magazine publishing techniques in the creation of this yearBOOK. Magazines also can be much cheaper than books because they are supported by advertising. To combine these assets into a great publication, we issued this yearBOOK in both magazine and book format at different prices.

CONTENTS

America's newest hobby is a handful of pure delight.

INTRODUCING HEDGEHOGS

Traveling backwards through time, we find all the animals that we are so familiar with as pets do not exist. Instead, they are merged together into earlier types of animals from which they evolved. One of the last animals that would be recognizable is the hedgehog. This small mammal, about the size of a guinea pig, waddled its way through history and into the hearts of a growing number of devotees. This text is designed to inform you of what a hedgehog is, and why has it suddenly become the new exotic pet of the Nineties.

HEDGEHOGS—LIVING FOSSILS

Hedgehogs are members of a group of animals known as insectivores. They are named for the fact that their diet consists largely of insects and other invertebrates (animals without a backbone). Insectivores were the first animals to develop a system of reproduction whereby their offspring were retained and nourished inside the body of the female. They were the first placental mammals. From them came all other mammals, such as dogs, cats, monkeys, cattle and even humans. They are thus fossils when compared to members of other mammalian orders. Today, the insectivores represent only about 9% of the mammals on our planet. When viewed in terms of number of species, this makes them the third most successful group. Table 1 compares insectivores with other popular mammalian orders. Generally, the insectivores are regarded as being rather primitive in their anatomy, which has changed little over the thousands of years since they began to evolve during the late Cretaceous period (about 100 million years ago).

The most well-known

> "Hedgehogs are classified as *insectivores* because they eat insects."

Insectivores were the first to evolve into placental mammals which nourished their young inside their bodies.

TABLE 1

Mammalian Orders to Show Species Numbers

Order		Number of Species
Rodentia:	Rats, Mice, Cavies, Squirrels, Gerbils, Chipmunks, Beavers, Hamsters and others	1,814
Chiroptera:	Bats	986
Insectivora:	Hedgehogs, Gymnures, Tenrecs, Shrews, Moles, Desmans	390
Marsupiala:	Kangaroos, Wallabies, Opossums, Wombats, Bandicoots, Marsupial Mice, and others	280
Carnivora:	Dogs, Cats, Bears, Raccoons, Weasels, Skunks, Otters, Civets, Genets and others	240
Primates:	Monkeys, Gibbons, Apes and Humans	233
Artiodactyla:	Pigs, Llamas, Camels, Deer, Cattle, Goats, Sheep, Antelopes, Giraffes, Hippos, others	211
Cetacea:	Whales, Dolphins, Porpoises	79
Lagomorpha:	Rabbits, Hares, Pikas	69
Perissodactyla:	Horses, Donkeys, Zebras, Rhinos, others	17

Note: The above are but 10 of the 21 mammalian orders. They account for all but 121 of the 4,400 species of mammals.

TABLE 2

Hedgehog Classification

Class
Mammalia

Order
Insectivora

Family **Erinaceidae:**	Hedgehogs & Gymnures (Moon Rats)	20 Species
Genera ***Erinaceus:***	Eurasian Hedgehogs	3 Species
Atelerix:	African Hedgehogs	4 Species
Paraechinus:	Desert Hedgehogs	3 Species
Hemiechinus:	Long-eared Desert Hedgehogs	4 Species
Family **Tenrecidae:**	Malagasy (Madagascar) Hedgehogs or Tenrecs	4 Species
	Five other families complete the order	

Note: *For any group of animals there is invariably more than one classification at any point in time. Zoologists may choose to differ on the exact standing and relationship of animal groups.*

insectivores are the shrews and moles. These are found all over the world. All insectivores share a number of features: a long snout, five digits on each foot, and 36-48 teeth of primitive type. Their cranial arrangements are broadly similar, and nearly all are nocturnal in habit. The skin is covered with close-lying hair in most species. There are variations found within differing insectivore groups. Hedgehogs display some of these variations.

Hedgehogs, along with their close relatives the tenrecs, evolved spines or quills as a means of defense. These have proved to be highly successful in protecting these animals from attack by predators. They cover the crown of the head, the back and the sides of the animal. The face, forehead, chest and underparts retain normal hair. Not common to insectivores, hedgehogs and their immediate kin have relatively large eyes and ears. These help to give them an especially appealing look. Most have a very short tail and short legs.

Hedgehogs are not related to other animals with spines, such as porcupines (which are rodents), and echidnas (marsupials). It is simply that these other mammals have developed a similar means of defending themselves in much the same way that many

animals have developed tusks as a means of defense, but are not related to each other (elephants, walruses and pigs). The way hedgehogs are classified by zoologists is shown in Table 2.

Hedgehogs are found in Europe, Africa and Asia, but are absent from the

A great photo but the spines on a hedgehog are not long...just sharp. They are NOT related to porcupines.

Americas and Australasia, though they have been introduced by humans to New Zealand. In the more northerly areas of their distribution they hibernate during the colder winters, but in the southerly regions they estivate. This means they will become torpid for a few weeks if it is very dry and there is little food to be had. During these natural bodily rhythms the heart beat and respiration rates drop dramatically, thus

conserving energy. However, under controlled temperature conditions, hedgehogs will remain active all year long.

THE POPULARITY OF HEDGEHOGS

Hedgehogs are not cuddly like rabbits or kittens, nor are they very intelligent, so cannot be taught tricks like dogs and parrots and they do not display any unusual color patterns. So, why have they become such rising stars on the pet scene? The basic answer is that they are very different from all of the other pets you are familiar with. After all, you can hardly cuddle a monitor lizard or a tarantula, but these animals are very popular. A potbellied pig is not everyone's idea of the "perfect pet," but they are loved and kept in many thousands of homes.

There are many benefits of owning a hedgehog. They are small, very quiet, and have a very appealing facial expression. They are not aggressive, and have virtually no body odor. Hedgehogs are quite happy waddling around your home in search of beetles, spiders and

Facing page:
Hedgehogs and their close relatives evolved quills and spines as a means of defense.

similar creatures that may be lurking in crevices and corners. They are easy pets to feed, and if handled on a regular basis will not roll up into a defensive ball of spines. Most people seeing a pet hedgehog for the first time are fascinated by them—especially children.

Hedgehogs are solitary creatures, and therefore do not mind being left alone for long periods of time. Indeed, they prefer to sleep during the day and will become active as the evening approaches–when you are at home to enjoy their company. They can be kept in an apartment where many other pets, such as dogs, noisy parrots, or potbellied pigs, may not be welcome! If you are unable to keep larger pets, or are looking for a little mammal that really is easy to keep and inoffensive, the hedgehog just might be the perfect pet for you.

> **"Hedgehogs are solitary pets and enjoy being left alone. They sleep during the day."**

You need a hand-tamed hedgehog to do this! Yes, they do have teeth and they can bite you, so be careful.

ACCOMMODATION

Hedgehogs are very easy pets to care for. In terms of their housing, there is a wide range of options from which to select and which would meet your budgetary needs. In general, the most important considerations of any pet accommodation are ease of cleaning, spaciousness, and durability. Although you can purchase your new pet's home on the day you obtain the hedgehog, it is usually wiser to purchase it in advance. This enables you to inspect the various options, and obtain the one you like best. This may not necessarily be available from the same store where you obtain the hedgehog.

WOODEN CAGES

The least costly hedgehog home would be an indoor rabbit hutch. Another option is a parakeet stock cage. These both have the advantage of offering your pet hedgehog privacy, yet giving you good frontage to view your pet easily when it leaves its nest box. Wooden cages are normally purchased unpainted, and it is up to you to do so. Be sure that the cage you decide upon is for parakeets, and not for finch-like birds. If you choose the rabbit hutch, it has the advantage of a much larger door. This makes it a little easier for you to gather up your pet. Both types of wooden cages normally have a sliding tray fitted to them for ease of cleaning.

> "Hedgehogs are very easy and inexpensive to care for since they are not aggressively active."

TRAVEL CRATES

There are many travel crates for you to choose

There are many different types of travel crates to choose from.

from with differing design features. They come in a range of colors, sizes, and prices. These crates are made from fiberglass or reinforced plastic. Their advantages are they are light, extremely easy to keep clean, and are very portable. Choose one of the larger sizes as these will provide more room for the nest box, and have sufficient space left for your hedgehog to move around in. Do bear in mind that even the largest travel crate is not spacious enough to provide your pet with a good exercise area. They merely make a very fine basic home. Your pet must be given as much time out of its accommodation as possible.

The design features to look for are that the door is fitted with a good fastening mechanism, is easy to take apart, and is made of a tough, durable material. Your local pet supply shop will carry a large selection of models from which you can choose.

THE NEST BOX & OTHER FITMENTS

Having settled on the housing, you will need a nest box for your new pet. You may inquire from your pet supply dealer as to which one will suit your new pet best. Whatever you decide upon, be certain it is durable and has a suitable sized entrance hole for your pet to enter.

One of the problems with plastic nest boxes is that they will tend to be pushed around the accommodation by your pet as it tries to look under them. By removing the lid from tote boxes it is more difficult for your pet to push it around. Another way of securing the nest box is to glue or screw retaining strips of plastic or wood to the housing floor so the nest box fits neatly into these.

You will also need a water dispenser. Those sold for hamsters are of an ideal size. They are designed to clip onto the cage door, making them easy to change. Initially, unless you are advised your pet is familiar with automatic

The pet travel crate is twice as wide and four times as long as the hedgehog.

dispensers, it would be wise also to have a small hamster water crock pot. This can always be used for food items once your pet has been seen to use the dispenser. You will need a couple of crock food pots,

A travel crate or animal carrier serves as a wonderful home for a hedgehog.

Small food cups can fit onto the cage door.

one for dry foods and the other for moist items, and maybe livefoods.

FLOOR COVERING

The most popular floor covering is pine wood shavings which can be purchased in various sized bags from your pet shop. Do not use cat litter as it is too harsh, and the dust in it is not good for your hedgehog's health. Likewise, sawdust is not recommended because it can cling to the ano-genital organs of these low bodied

animals and may cause irritation. Natural plant matter cat litter is a relatively new product and will work fine as a floor covering. Garden soil may seem a good idea but it carries the risk of introducing parasites to your pet.

Garden potting soil, however, is safe and should not cause any problems. Indeed, your pet will forage over this, much as it would in the wild, if you place a few food items in it. If the housing is large enough, you can place a small litter tray into this and it will be used by some pets.

Facing page: Hedgehogs require some area for exercise. They are not active but they do need a minimum of activity.

Exercise wheels in glass aquariums are ideal for hedgehogs.

THE INDOOR RUN

If space permits you can provide your hedgehog with its own exercise area by placing its home in an indoor run. This allows it to waddle around at its own leisure rather than just when you are home to supervise its movements outside of its accommodation. The pen is easily made by stapling weldwire to a wooden frame. The height should be a minimum of about 38cm (15in). It is best to place a weldwire cover over the run because these little pets are able to climb up the sides of weldwire and might just escape. Alternatively, make the side from panels so your pet cannot climb. Place the side panels on a painted wooden floor that is covered as for the housing floor.

The indoor pen can be made more interesting by including rocks, logs and other items that your pet will enjoy investigating and waddling around and over. If you do provide an indoor run then you can feed the hedgehog in this, rather than in its crate or hutch.

SITING THE HOUSING

Hedgehogs, like any other pets, quickly suffer if placed in drafty locations. Likewise, their home should not be sited where the temperature fluctuates—such as near heating units, or where it is exposed to direct sunlight for long periods. Nor should it be placed where the temperature falls below

Hedgehogs like to investigate. A simple cloth napkin becomes a toy for them.

about 55°F(13°C) otherwise the pet will go into a state of inactivity. This is where it becomes rather inactive and sleepy. The ideal temperature will be within the range of 60-75°F(16-24°C) for the African species. These are the ones

Closeup of an exercise wheel being utilized by a hedgehog.

This small plastic box is NOT suitable for the long term home of hedgehogs.

you are most likely to obtain.

Hedgehogs can cope with somewhat higher temperatures than the upper limit quoted here, but

Plastic food containers should not be too high

it should be remembered that in their native homelands they are active at night when the temperature has fallen from that of the daytime. They will normally find a shaded spot and sleep through the heat of the day.

Hedgehogs are very clean animals with almost no odor.

ROUTINE CLEANING

In order to ensure that your pet remains healthy, and its home does not smell, you should clean its cage at least once per week and remove and trash all floor covering material. Once empty, use bleach to disinfect the home then rinse this with clean water so there are no residual chemicals left in the accommodation. Food pots should be washed daily, water dispensers once per week. In between full cleans you should remove fecal matter on a daily basis. If you keep two or more hedgehogs, be sure that food and water pots are returned to the same cages—number the cages and the pots.

Hedgehogs are very clean living animals with almost no odor. If their home ever smells, it is because the owner has neglected routine cleaning.

Clean the cage at least once a week with a complete change of the bedding and a sterilization of the cage itself with a bleach like Clorox.

CHOOSING A HEDGEHOG

The factors you need to consider before purchasing your hedgehog are its legal status, age, sex, color, disposition, health, source, and price. A little time spent pondering these matters will be rewarded by your taking home the pet most suited to your needs.

HEDGEHOG SPECIES

Before discussing the various topics mentioned, a few words with respect to the hedgehog species you are likely to find on sale may be of value. When hedgehogs first started to become popular as pets, there were a number of species imported into the USA. Distinction between these was not made and they were sold as African hedgehogs, Pygmy hedgehogs, or Dwarf hedgehogs. Of the 14 hedgehog species, the Long-eared hedgehogs of the genus *Hemiechinus* can be readily identified by their long ears. It is more difficult to accurately identify members of the other ten species.

One of the problems that comes when species are not

The hedgehogs sold as pets went under such names as *African, pygmy or dwarf hedgehogs.*

Consider age, sex, color, price and health before deciding on your hedgehog purchase.

There are several color varieties of hedgehogs. Regardless of the color, hedgehogs' personalities are a product of their environment.

Before you buy a hedgehog, be sure
it can legally be kept in your home.
Don't fall in love with a hedgehog
and have to get rid of it because of
the local, state or county regulations
about wild animals!

readily identified is that they are hybridized. This makes matters more complicated because it creates intergrades that may display features of two or more formerly distinct species. This situation persists in these pets, though generally those on offer will be of the genus *Atelerix*, the African hedgehogs. These, apart from the common names already stated, may also be sold under the name of white-bellied hedgehogs. It has to be said that most hedgehogs may have white underparts, so you should not read too much into the common name applied to the pets on offer.

undecided. As far as can be ascertained, they can be kept in all other states. However, each state, indeed each county, sets its own bylaws. It is a case of your making inquiries with pet shops, your vet, the USDA, and your local town hall.

The hedgehog is classified as a non-dangerous exotic animal. Some localities have rules for any animal classed as exotic. They may not allow them, or they may require you to have a permit, or meet other requirements. When a new pet arrives on the scene many authorities are not sure themselves how to interpret the regulations. You may need to petition

The ideal age to purchase a pet hedgehog is eight weeks.

AGE TO PURCHASE
The age at which it is best to obtain a hedgehog will be influenced by the reason you want it. If it is to be a single pet then the ideal age will be when it is about eight weeks old. At this time it will have been weaned from its mother's milk and will be eating and living independent of her. Although hedgehogs may be sold at a younger age (four to six weeks in some instances) you are not advised to acquire such a youngster as it may not have been fully weaned and problems may result.

If you are seeking breeding stock, the youngest age would be approximately four to five months for a female. At this age she would still be too young for breeding, but it gives you a couple of months to get to know her, and for her to settle down to

> " **The hedgehog is a non-dangerous exotic animal. There are many laws on the books dealing with *exotic* animals. Check with your local police chief.** "

LEGAL STATUS
The very first thing you must do before making the decision to purchase a hedgehog is to find out whether or not it can legally be kept in your state and locality. At the time of writing, California, Arizona and Alaska have ruled that they cannot be kept as pets. Imprisonment and fines can result if you keep them in these states. Colorado is

them to change the wording in order to accommodate the pet. You are advised to contact other local hedgehog owners, or would-be owners, then seek help from NAHA (North American Hedgehog Association). Never break the rules as this will not help your cause. Work with officials in order to gain suitable status for these pets.

This is a normal agouti-colored hedgehog. It has the colors of a wild rabbit, a wild cat or a wild rat.

is placed somewhat forward of its position in most other popular pets. The female's urogenital organs are separate, but close together when compared to those of the male.

The hedgehog has a life span of about six to eight years under captive conditions and it is entirely possible that this may be exceeded with proper care and accommodation.

HEDGEHOG COLORS

The normal or wild coloration of the hedgehog is variable, but is based around the agouti pattern. This means that the spines are banded in yellow, white, brown or black. This color pattern is seen in wild rabbits, cats, mice and many other mammals, including the South American agouti, for which it is named. Such a pattern

> **" Both males and females make equally fine pets; if you have more than one hedgehog, keep them separated. "**

your home. Once over six months of age she can be bred. A male can be test bred at about the same age.

THE CHOICE OF SEX

It does not matter which sex you obtain if you are looking to purchase a pet. Both make fine little companions. You should accommodate them in separate quarters if you have two or more pets so there will be no possibility of your having unwanted litters or unnecessary fighting. Males, under any circumstance, will not live together in harmony.

By inspecting the underparts you can readily identify the sexes. The male's penis is evident as it provides an excellent camouflage against the background in which these animals live.

However, some individuals may show a predominance of black in their pattern, others may display more white (Snowflakes). Yet others may show both extremes in the same animal and appear black and white. These are called polka dots in the hedgehog fancy. There are also creams, which are really very pale browns rather than true creams in the genetic sense. The underbelly color is normally white, but this too can range through brown to almost black. The mask may also range from almost white to almost black.

Color and pattern mutations will no doubt appear as hedgehogs are bred on a larger scale, and it is reported that albinos are already evident. An albino is pure white with red eyes, though some may show slight pigmentation (yellowish) in the fur. What you should be aware of is that there is a world of difference between a color that is within the normal range of the hedgehog, and one that is a genuine mutant.

From the pet perspective this is of no matter, but for the potential breeder it is significant. A dark looking hedgehog mated to a similar specimen may produce any of the colors that are normal for that species. But

If you can handle a hedgehog, it is easy to ascertain its sex. The male organ is located relatively high from the anal pore.

"It's easy to select a pet hedgehog since sex, color and age are not considerations. Only health and price are important unless you want to breed."

A female hedgehog has her reproductive and excretory orifices close together. If your hedgehog isn't tame, it isn't easy to ascertain an animal's sex.

a mutant black to a mutant black will produce its own color, much as a true albino to albino will only produce albino. This may not be so with individuals that are simply very light colored (almost white) examples.

DISPOSITION

It is very important that you obtain a pet with a good disposition. This will make life much easier for you than if you have to devote many hours to taming your little hedgehog. A pet that is already very tame and quite happy to be lifted up without curling itself into a defensive ball, or charging you with its head spines, is definitely worth the extra dollars its seller will want for it.

It is not possible to say that hedgehogs displaying aggressive temperaments are the result of poor breeding, though this could be the case in some instances. What is more

> **" Buy a hand-tamed hedgehog, even if the price is much higher than a wild one. "**

true to say is that these pets instinctively take up defensive postures when they feel threatened. Unlike most other pets that simply try to run away from fearful situations, the hedgehog evolved to stay put and let its spines dissuade potential aggressors.

This is the way a hedgehog should be offered for sale.

The ideal sequence of events with hedgehogs is that the breeder will devote some time to hand taming their youngsters so they can be handled when they reach the pet store. The store itself should spend some time gentling these infants so they remain tame. Hedgehogs need constant handling until they are really tame, after which they will remain in this state with regular petting.

It must be stressed that if a pet shop is selling very tame hedgehogs, you should be prepared to pay extra for these. Do not compare them with cheaper specimens elsewhere that will not let you handle them. Even tame pets may show some apprehension at being handled over the first day or two, because hedgehogs relate very much to their surroundings. Once they are settled and become familiar with your daily routine they quickly lose initial fears.

SELECT A HEALTHY PET

Nothing can be worse than purchasing a pet only to find that within days it becomes ill and transforms an exciting time into one of worry and regret. You can largely avoid this scenario by ensuring you only purchase a healthy little pet. Start by viewing as many pet shops as you can so you can compare the conditions the pets are living under. These should be warm, spacious, and clean. Each cage should have its water vessel filled, with evidence that the floor covering is being cleaned on a regular basis.

Look for any signs of liquid fecal matter—that of a healthy hedgehog is an elongated dark brown pellet. Young hedgehogs should ideally be accommodated in their own cage, not housed with others. They are capable of breeding from a very young

The younger the hedgehog, the sharper the spines. This old man has spines which are almost dull.

age so it is wrong to leave mixed sexes together once they are weaned. Females of the same litter may live amicably together while they are youngsters, but mature females, and all males, should be housed independent of each other to avoid the risk of fighting.

If you are satisfied with the living quarters, the hedgehogs should be inspected. This may be difficult because they prefer to curl into a ball during the daytime. The sales assistant may be able to coax one to open up so you can view it. The eyes of a healthy pet are round and clear, and show no signs of weeping. The nose is just moist, not totally dry, and not running. Part the fur in the opposite direction that it lies to check that there are no signs of parasites, such as lice, fleas or ticks.

There should be no areas of bald fur, nor signs of lumps or abrasions. The front feet will have five digits, the rear four or five depending on the species. The anal region should be clean, showing no signs of congealed fecal matter, nor staining that would suggest diarrhea. The spines of babies are very sharp, these becoming a little less so as the animal matures.

Although the spines do come out periodically there is no mass shedding. If the animal is shedding profusely, it is not in good health. If you do have the opportunity to see the pet

walking, this should be of a side-to-side waddling nature, but certainly not a limping action.

If the pet passes your physical examination you can assume it is healthy. Even so it would be wise to have your vet examine it as soon as possible after you get it home, or request a certificate of health from the seller (for which you must be prepared to pay extra). Hedgehogs are very hardy little animals so if you have the slightest

Hedgehogs are best kept isolated. In this way you can control both breeding and fighting.

"Hedgehogs do NOT shed seasonally. They lose a few spines every week or so. More than this means trouble."

doubts as to the condition of any on offer you should seek out an alternative. A little shopping inconvenience is far better than a lot of subsequent unhappiness!

SOURCES OF HEDGEHOGS

If you are looking for a companion hedgehog the best place to purchase from is a pet shop in your locality. From this you can obtain your hedgehog related foods and appliances, and can go back to the source should you have inquiries or any problems. You are also able to see exactly what you are buying, and the conditions it is living under. If you live in a rural area that is far away from a pet shop you should make contact with NAHA (North American Hedgehog Association) who will be able to supply you with a list of registered breeders from whom you can purchase in confidence via mail order. No other source is advisable. If the pet shop of your choice does not have a hedgehog at the time you want it they can obtain a nice one for you via a NAHA breeder, so one way or the other these are the only two recommended sources. As with any 'new' pet, the hedgehog has attracted a number of disreputable people who see it as an opportunity to make some quick cash. They advertise stock they do not always have, and at prices that

Pulling a hedgehog from its day long nap is hardly fun for the hedgehog, so be careful!

may not reflect the current value of a sound typical pet.

If you purchase via mail order be sure you have a written contract stating exactly what you are purchasing before parting with a deposit, or the full amount. Ask the seller to advise you who their vet is, and insist that the pet comes with a signed health certificate by that vet or clinic. Contact the vet in question before sending any cash. There is nothing wrong in checking out the reputation of a source. No reputable seller will mind this at all.

THE PRICE OF A HEDGEHOG

There is no set price that a hedgehog will cost. Prices reflect a number of factors as follows:

1. An eight week old baby of normal color will be the least expensive, the females being somewhat more desirable, thus a little more expensive.

2. A young adult boar will normally be a little cheaper than its female counterpart, but more costly than a very young specimen.

3. A young proven breeding female (sow) will be more costly than an unproven sow.

4. A hedgehog which

displays very light, very dark, or patterned coloration will be more valuable than the normal agouti color already discussed.

5. Any hedgehog that is really tame will be more

Highly marked, hand-tamed, proven sow is the most expensive kind of hedgehog.

costly than if it has yet to be tamed.

As a ballpark guide, prices from pet shop to pet shop should not vary tremendously. They should have competitive prices.

The more unusual colors will command higher prices than the normal ones, and genuine mutational colors will be even more costly as they arrive, and while they are in short supply. Reliable breeding females will always be the most expensive within their color category (and more so if they are known to be good foster mothers). Quality breeding males of proven fecundity, and which stamp their type on their progeny, will again always be worth a goodly price.

You are not advised to purchase expensive breeding hedgehogs until you have gained experience in managing them, and have decided whether or not they are the right pets for you and your family. If you diligently follow the advice given in this chapter you should obtain exactly the right hedgehog for your needs. This should be a fine healthy specimen that will share many years of happiness with you.

> **❝ There is no set price for a hedgehog. The price depends on age, health, sex and tameness. Don't buy an expensive animal until you have some experience with them. ❞**

A hedgehog is a hedgehog. It's not a dog, cat, rat or hamster. Its needs are different than most familiar family pets.

HEDGEHOGS AS PETS

Hedgehogs are not like other small mammals that are usually kept as pets, nor should you ever compare them with such. Always bear in mind they are what they are. They should not be regarded as dogs, cats, hamsters, or rabbits, but simply as hedgehogs with their own little ways, needs, and characters.

LIFE IN THE WILD

To help us understand the animals we share our homes with, we should know a little bit about their lifestyle in the wild. Hedgehogs are nocturnal (nighttime) and crepuscular (dawn and dusk) in their activities. They do not roam about during daylight hours unless they are forced to for some reason. For most of their lives they are solitary creatures that come together only for the purposes of mating.

Although they do not establish and defend territories, they avoid their own kind and come together in numbers only if the situation is abnormal. Such an instance is where they may live in close proximity to a food source, such as human garbage dumps, or around human settlements.

The hedgehog's home is a simple structure. It will either burrow under a pile of leaves, or a low lying bush, or it will fashion a shallow burrow just large enough to nestle into. It may also take up residence in any hollow created by another animal, or a rock crevice. If it lives, as many do, near human homes, it will happily take up residence under a shed or similar outbuilding. In Britain, Mainland Europe, and other areas where hedgehogs are indigenous, they are often welcomed into gardens because they will eat slugs, snails, insects and many other

> " Hedgehogs are nocturnal. They do not roam about during the daylight hours unless they are forced to do so."

creatures that most people do not want around their homes.

Often, residents will put scraps of food and bread and milk out to encourage the hedgehog to remain in their garden. But such tolerance does not extend to encouraging these animals into homes because they are associated with having lice, fleas and ticks. These parasites will not be a problem to your pet hedgehog because it will not be living in the wild, so will be no more risk to these unwanted pests than a cat or dog.

The diet of the wild hedgehog is very cosmopolitan. It is a very active little animal that is constantly on the move at night searching for food. It is very much an opportunist forager. A typical menu would include worms, beetles, fallen birds' eggs, snails, newborn mice and reptiles, baby frogs, moths, spiders, carrion and any discarded human foods. It may eat a small amount of vegetable and plant matter, but these are not major diet items.

It has few natural enemies, but these include foxes, rats, polecats, large birds of prey, and, of course, human beings. The tight ball of spines it presents to attackers is very often sufficient to ensure it is able to deter most aggressors. When touched it will "jump" upwards just enough so that its spines make contact with

Hedgehogs are solitary animals. They only meet at feeding places, especially garbage dumps, where they feed.

whatever is touching it. When on the move and approached from the front, it will lower its cap of head spines to face the aggressor and make a tiny charge, again, just enough to spike anything within one half inch of its head. When contented it lowers its spines so they lie flat against its body and head.

approached, they will make a rapid clicking sound. They are also able to make a low grunting sound when foraging. When badly frightened or hurt, they squeal in a high pitched manner. Finally, what is best described as a purring sound is used when something interests them.

SELF-ANOINTING

A rather unusual, if not bizarre, habit displayed by hedgehogs is that known as self-anointing. No one is really sure why they do this. What happens is that the hedgehog will sniff or lick at something—which can be as diverse as sweat on your hands to perfume, to fecal matter, to any of many

Hedgehogs are inquisitive and when they raise the head spines it might be a manifestation of a defensive gesture.

VOCALIZATIONS

Hedgehogs are able to make a number of sounds to express their mood of the moment. They issue a sort of sneezing, snorting sound when they are apprehensive about anything approaching their head. If they are in a defensive ball and are

> **"Hedgehogs can make sounds which vary from sneezing to snorting to clicking. When they are frightened they squeal."**

other chemical smells. This sniffing elicits frothy saliva to form in the mouth. This is then deposited onto the hedgehog's spines via its long tongue.

It is said to be part of a sexual sequence by some experts; others feel it is some form of defensive mechanism based on the fact that these animals have been seen to anoint after rubbing against toads known to carry toxins in their skin. Another theory is that it may be a form of phlegming, a combined smell-taste action seen in dogs, cats and other mammals, and which involves the Jacobson's organ situated in the roof of the mouth.

In the wild it is said to be exhibited only during the breeding season, which supports the sexual connections. However, there are hedgehogs that have been known to commence this when they scent anything unusual, then not do it for weeks. Is it possibly some form of familiarization ritual, or is it a combination of things? Certainly, it is interesting and worthy of your own thoughts when you see it for yourself.

HAND TAMING

It may be that the hedgehog you purchase is not fully hand tame and, if this is so, the following comments will be found useful. The spines of these pets are sharp and can inflict pain if you do not

> "Self anointing is a weird hedgehog characteristic. Simulated by an uncommon scent, it froths at the mouth and the froth is spread over its spines by the hedgehog's long tongue."

handle the hedgehog carefully. Small children should not be allowed to try to pick up a hedgehog. If

The usual hedgehog home is a shallow tunnel dug into soft earth. Don't try to imitate it in your home.

they were pricked this would prompt them to drop the pet, and maybe lose interest in it. If the pet is mishandled it merely reinforces its desire not to be handled.

Before trying to handle your pet it should be allowed a day or two to

settle down into its new home, become accustomed to its feeding routine, and to the sound of your voice. Some owners use a wide plastic spatula to slide under their pet's body, then transfer the pet onto their lap or hand.

Others have worn a tough leather glove on one hand and slowly approach the side of the hedgehog. Its reaction is to lower the spines of its body towards the perceived aggressor, and to snort. I then gently, but firmly, push my gloved hand under its body and lift—at the same time talking to it in a soft voice. It is then placed onto the opposite hand, which should be ungloved, and then onto the lap. Once in this position these pets rarely become belligerent. Usually they will start to sniff your hands and clothes.

When this method has been used a number of times your pet can usually be lifted without the need of

> "Use a tough leather glove when handling hedgehogs!"

The spines on hedgehogs are sharp and can inflict painful wounds. Children should not be allowed to handle hedgehogs without protective gloves.

You shouldn't handle a hedgehog without a stout glove.

the glove, but you must still do it with caution until you are very confident of its reaction— and it of yours. With daily handling, hedgehogs become more and more confident about being picked up, to the point they will not snort or attempt to resist your actions.

The gloved hand is preferred because this enables you to confidently lift your pet without the risk of being spiked and, out of reflex, drop the pet. At the same time, the ungloved hand that receives it enables it to become familiar with your scent. Hedgehogs rarely bite, but if they attempt to do so your gloved hand will protect you from the little nip involved and, again, remove the risk you might pull away and drop your pet. This would tend to encourage it to repeat what it did the first time!

Occasionally, your pet might start to lick your

finger and then suddenly nip it. This is not an aggressive act but merely a finding out process on your pet's behalf. Children should not be allowed to poke their fingers through the weldwire door of their pet's home. This may result in the pet licking them, then suddenly nipping!

As stated earlier in this chapter, hedgehogs are hedgehogs, not little puppies. But even pups and kittens tend to nip while they are babies and

> **"The spines on a hedgehog are sharp, strong and dangerous. If you are injured, get treatment as quickly as possible as there might be dangerous infections as a consequence."**

learning that fingers are parts of your body and not food items! Once a pet hedgehog is well tamed it is as gentle a pet as any other, and can be confidently picked up without any fears at all. At such times its spines will remain flat against its

body, a sure sign it is contented and unafraid. The key to success with hedgehogs is that they must be handled on a regular basis—which does not mean being constantly woken from their sleep, but by daily handling before or a little after feeding time.

LITTER TRAINING

If your hedgehog has a large crate or indoor run you can try to litter train it. From the day you obtain it retain a pellet of its fecal matter along with a spoonful of urinated floor covering. Place this into a litter tray containing a floor covering different to the one used for main floor area. Be sure the latter area is free of fecal matter. Also, keep the litter tray as far away from the food and water containers as possible.

If you attend to this matter diligently your pet will prefer to use its litter tray than to soil the floor. Once it is seen to be using the tray as hoped, you must not then leave fecal matter in it but keep it very clean. Your pet's action of using the tray as a toilet will of itself become an internalized reinforcer that prompts it to use the tray. It is also important that the main floor area is kept clean of the occasional fouling otherwise this will undo that achieved initially.

However, hedgehogs do not defecate as often as most other small pets, so they are much easier to keep clean.

SECURITY

Your pet will enjoy a romp around your living room, or wherever you decide it can be allowed to exercise freely. The following are a few useful tips. Hedgehogs are small animals; they are extremely inquisitive and possess a very good sense of hearing and smell. If they hear the noise of an insect behind a washing machine, or similar heavy appliance, they will try to get at it because this represents a tasty morsel! If they scent a food item in a dark cupboard full of all the things you have always intended to clear out, but never have, they will find a way into this and happily settle down for a nap after eating any bugs and beetles found.

They will clamber into flower baskets, hide behind the sofa, or waddle happily under a bed. They will enjoy sleeping in a pile of clothes waiting to be washed, or merrily munch away on any appealing foods at floor level in a pantry. With such dangers in mind you should safeguard against them, or only let your pet run freely while you are keeping an eye on it. In the early hours of

The spines are the hedgehog's primary defense. Hedgehogs are able to raise the spines in a defensive posture, or lay them down when they are calm. Treat these spines with great respect!

evening, before the sun goes down, it is fine to let your pet amble around your garden—providing you are constantly watching it so it does not find somewhere to hide. It will enjoy foraging around the base of trees and shrubs where it will no doubt find numerous little delicacies to eat. It cannot be stressed enough that you must keep an eye on your pet, otherwise it can so easily hide from your sight and be lost.

THE OUTDOOR ENCLOSURE

An alternative means of exercise is to erect an outdoor enclosure, complete with a stout wooden or similar nest box. In this enclosure your pet can exercise freely during the night, and in total safety during the warmer spring through late summer days. The floor of the run should be paved or concreted so it can easily be kept clean, and to prevent the pet from burrowing under the sides. It can contain a large rooting box filled with potting soil and morsels of food. You can landscape the run with rocks, logs, and other places to explore. If the run has a secure weld wire covering, your pet will be safe from potential predators. It will really enjoy its time in this little ecosystem. It must be returned indoors during the cold months.

Hedgehogs are not heavy and their weight alone will not enable their spines to pierce your skin...but don't take any chances. Always use a glove.

FEEDING HEDGEHOGS

Hedgehogs are not difficult pets to feed in respect of their nutritional needs, nor do they consume large quantities of food, so they are relatively economical. However, some can be rather picky, others being less picky. They must be fed on an individual basis according to their appetite and condition. It is important to find out from the person who sold you your pet exactly what the hedgehog has been eating. Maintain this diet for a few days and then widen the scope, if this is needed, based on what follows in this chapter.

FEEDING TYPE

Your new pet is scientifically classed as an omnivore (will eat foods of both plant and animal origin), but with a strong leaning to being a carnivore (flesh eater). It is best that you feed them as you would a carnivore, such as a dog, cat, or ferret; however, often try a few vegetable and plant foods to see if you can interest them in these. A hedgehog's wild habitat diet is made up largely of invertebrate animals. Under domestic conditions you can substitute numerous other foods in place of these, though a few invertebrates will be relished and beneficial to their good health.

VARIETY IS THE KEY

A diet that is as varied as possible serves a two-fold purpose. For one, it greatly reduces the chance that a needed ingredient is missing from the diet, and secondly, feeding the pet becomes easier because it will be less picky in its eating habits (it has a wide selection to choose from). Of course, all animals tend to have certain foods that are preferred to others, so it's a case of balancing the items so that it cannot gorge itself on a favored item, thus ignoring other valuable foods.

THE FOOD GROUPS

All foods contain some ingredients from each of the food groups. Of course, certain foods are richer in given ingredients than others. Depending on the animal eating them, some are more, and some less, valuable to them as a food item. The digestive system of the hedgehog evolved to

> **"Most hedgehogs are not fussy eaters, but yours might be."**

Hedgehogs require a varied diet to be sure they get all the ingredients they need. This is best accomplished by mashing everything together and offering it in a single feeding dish.

Baby hedgehogs which are hand-fed, become the most tame and are the most desirable as pets.

cope very well with proteins and fats—flesh in its various forms. It is much less able to digest plant material, which is mainly composed of carbohydrates.

Carnivores are able to oxidize proteins down to their basic amino acids. They then rebuild these into the sort of proteins they need. Herbivores (plant eaters, such as rabbits and cattle) have a totally different digestive system. They are able to break down the cellulose walls of plants and utilize the small amounts of protein in the plant—but they need to eat **a lot** more than carnivores in order to obtain their protein needs. Proteins are thus the building blocks of the body. Fats provide a rich reserve energy source, but are

essentially used to provide insulation against the cold, and to buffer the muscles and bones from knocks. Carbohydrates are the most common (thus least expensive) foods of all. They provide energy for day-to-day muscular activity. Your pet must also have certain quantities of vitamins, minerals, and water. Each of these is

> **66 Hedgehogs must have vitamins, minerals and water, just as all other animals with backbones. Which vitamins and minerals it needs and how much of each is yet to be ascertained. 99**

found in all foods, but some foods contain more of them than others.

In the wild, a hedgehog will consume the entire

prey on which it feeds, including whatever is in that animal's digestive tract. In this way it obtains all of the ingredients just discussed. Under captive conditions it may miss out on certain vitamins, in particular, because it may not be receiving whole prey items. This is why vitamin supplements have become so popular. An excess of vitamins, however, can be as dangerous as a lack of them. Their need must therefore be based on what variety of foods, and what items, are being eaten by your pet. If it takes a wide-ranging diet, including invertebrates, and maybe a little fruit or fish liver oils, it is unlikely it will ever lack vitamins. If it becomes a picky eater then supplements may prove beneficial under veterinary advice.

If you hand feed the baby hedgehog, clean it up afterwards or the uneaten food might serve as a feeding site for unwanted bacteria.

SUGGESTED DIET ITEMS

There is a wide range of foods that you can give to your hedgehogs, so the following are but some suggestions from different owners. Try a selection of them and observe those eaten by your pet, and in what quantity. This means that you must spend time

Unfortunately, pet shops do not offer a special hedgehog food, but they do have special foods which satisfy the hedgehog's basic needs. Since new foods are marketed monthly, ask your local pet supplier which food he recommends.

watching your pet eat which becomes important should your hedgehog fall ill and require coaxing into maintaining a food intake.

Meat in its various forms is always relished by hedgehogs. Beef, either raw or cooked, and minced or cut into small slices, is the way to prepare these items. Give them raw and cooked but be sure the quality is good—fit for human consumption. Poultry, such as chicken and turkey, is well liked. Again, this can be fed raw or cooked.

Canned dog or cat foods are excellent and have been fortified with vitamins after the cooking process, so will make very good basic diet items. Some hedgehogs will not, however, show much interest in these if they are receiving meats as discussed. Dry cat biscuits, liked by most hedgehogs are a handy small size that your pet can easily get into its mouth to munch.

Cheese of various kinds, but especially cottage cheese, is enjoyed by most hedgehogs. Slivers of boiled, cooked white fish will be taken by some pets, ignored by others. Sausages, either cooked or raw, will again appeal according to the sausage type and the taste preference of your pet. Hamburgers are in the same category as sausages. Egg yolk, raw or scrambled, is another protein-rich food.

It is not essential that your pet have livefoods, but they are very much liked and therefore recommended. You do not need to cultivate these yourself because today there are many companies who do this messy job on a commercial basis. Mealworms are nutritious and easy to keep in your refrigerator. Give

Canned dog food is excellent for hedgehogs and has proven satisfactory.

❝ Give your hedgehog human quality food. Experiment with raw and cooked chicken, turkey or beef. Hedgehogs are not very active and are small so their feed requirements are inexpensive. ❞

approximately 3-5 at one feeding, two or three times a week, assuming other meats, as discussed, are being fed.

Maggots are best avoided due to their association with botulism. In any case they offer limited nutritional value. Your local pet shop will have a selection of other small worms and invertebrates that can form part of the diet. Be sure to keep these in sawdust or cornmeal for a while before feeding them to your hedgehog so they void the contents of their gut into this. Do not feed color dyed invertebrates from angling stores because the dye may be toxic if stored in the body.

Bread soaked in milk may be welcomed by some pets and of no interest to others, the same applies to small diced fruits, such as apple, peach, apricot, fig, and strawberries. By all means offer your pet selections from the extensive list of possible fruits and vegetables. A drop or two of any fish liver oil will contain many vitamins, as will liver, but give these sparingly otherwise they can easily cause stomach upsets and diarrhea.

MASHES

One way to coax your pet to accept a new food item is to include a small quantity of it within a mash containing favored items. Use a cereal product as the

You can obtain some live food from your pet shop. Mealworms make great meals for hedgehogs.

Some hedgehogs let you know when they are hungry by constantly going to their feeding dish.

base and add to this a range of protein-rich foods, as discussed, together with just a touch of fruits and vegetables. Moisten (not soak!) with beef extract and serve. You will need to do a degree of experimenting to obtain the right balance of ingredients versus acceptance, but when this is achieved you can mix larger quantities and store them in the refrigerator. With a dry or moist mash your pet cannot avoid tasting certain items as it picks out the ones it likes best. It may then develop a liking for a previously ignored item.

HOW OFTEN TO FEED

The number of times your pet will need feeding is directly related to how much food it is given at each feed. The hedgehog is most active as evening approaches, and overnight, so this is when its main meal should be provided. If you are an early riser it can receive its first meal at this time. If you are not, then it is suggested you feed at about 6pm then top this up before you retire, so there is food available for the pet overnight.

The amount of food per meal will be influenced by the quality of the foods given. The richer the meal is in quality proteins, the less food will be consumed. As a guide, you are advised to prepare a varied meal and see how much your

pet eats. If the dish is emptied at a single sitting then there was not enough given. If some is left you can reduce the size of the next meal. By this method of trial and error you will quickly come to know the appetite of your particular pet.

Your hedgehog's food intake will vary somewhat from day to day, just as yours does. Some days your pet will not eat as much, other days it will want more. Use your best

judgment and you will not go far wrong. If your pet is recovering from an illness, it will need more food. The growing youngster must also have a growing amount per meal. The breeding female will consume much more than normal as she approaches parturition, and even more once the babies are born. The active pet will eat more than one which is confined and under-exercised (but it is hoped this will never be the case!).

If you put your hedgehogs together just for feeding, you might be looking for trouble. Hedgehogs fight over food and reproduction.

"Feed your hedgehogs at 6pm and then add more, if required, before you retire. This should last overnight. Hedgehogs eat at night."

Many hedgehogs love eggs. It's best for YOU to crack the egg open. Eggs are good for satisfying your hedgehog's protein and cholesterol needs.

BREEDING

Potential hedgehog breeders will fall into one of two broad groups of people. There are those which have never bred any species of small mammals, such as rabbits, mice, hamsters or guinea pigs, and those that have. If you are one of those that have never bred any small mammal before, you are strongly advised to gain practical experience in keeping hedgehogs before you consider the possibility of breeding them. If you have bred other small mammals on any sort of regular basis, you should be able to breed hedgehogs without any major problems, provided you follow the advice given in this chapter.

BREEDING CONSIDERATIONS

If you stand back from the initial enthusiasm of breeding hedgehogs, you will consider the practical realities of what this entails. It can be divided into the following areas.

1. Having the time to devote to the needs of owning numerous hedgehogs in a breeding program.

2. Having the available accommodation for the breeding stock and their offspring.

3. Obtaining the initial breeding animals and planning a program.

4. Effecting a mating and knowing the biology of the breeding process—practical breeding.

5. Deciding which youngsters to sell and how to go about this.

THE TIME FACTOR

You should not think of breeding any pet unless you are sure you have the available spare time to devote to the breeding animals and their offspring. The more hedgehogs you have, the more time must be spent on general chores—cleaning and feeding. Once the babies are born their demands on your time start to rise dramatically. This is not so immediately, but comes as they start moving around outside the nest box.

This is when the process of bonding to humans commences. This is a critical period with hedgehogs because these pets are not naturally social by nature, as are most other pet mammals. They require much time spent with them so that by the time they are ready to go to their new homes they are very confident about being handled. This aspect is often downgraded by breeders who seek to breed high numbers, rather than maintain a smaller herd whose offspring are very well-socialized to humans—which takes much time.

ACCOMMODATION NEEDS

Each breeding boar and sow will require their own accommodation. A nest box will be essential. Once the youngsters have been weaned they are best placed into their own sex groups until they are ready to be sold. You can keep them together as litters until they are sold but, depending when this is, there is the theoretical possibility that young females might be mated as they reach sexual maturity at a very young age.

Youngsters can also cohabit quite amicably if they have a very large nursery pen and are well fed, but there is always the risk of squabbling and injury with each passing week. Once the hoglets have attained three months of age, they are best housed in their own accommodation.

OBTAINING BREEDING STOCK

If you live reasonably close to an established breeder, there is no need to obtain a boar until you have established a small herd. Initially, one of the breeder's boars can mate all your sows, and after this you can either retain a boar from your own litters, or continue for a while to use the services of the best boars in your area. This is utilizing your best options until you see the exact boar you want. Do not commit to more than one to three sows because you may lose interest in the hobby as it becomes too overwhelming too quickly. This way you limit your time and investment while you decide to what level, or not, you wish to involve yourself.

Be sure that your breeding sows are tractable and from a reputable source. It is also best if these are proven breeders. They will be more costly to purchase, but the investment is worthwhile. If you start with a herd of three sows you should try to obtain these from unrelated lines. This enables you to develop independent lines rather than having all the genes in the one basket, speaking figuratively.

The value of this policy will become apparent if you care to make a study of genetics and breeding policies. Even after having established a successful herd, there is always merit in having a distantly related second or third line that can be used as a safe outcross if this is needed. This is noted on the assumption that you will carefully linebreed rather than conduct an

unplanned mating program.

If you wish to be a very serious breeder you must study mating systems so you are able to move towards a true breeding objective, rather than merely produce hedgehogs to sell.

PRACTICAL BREEDING INFORMATION

Allow your breeding sows

The male's sex organ is located about an inch above its anal pore.

to settle in for a week or two before you have them mated. Alternatively, if you are purchasing proven breeders, you could have one or two of the sows mated prior to collecting them. This is only suggested if you already have good small mammal breeding experience, when you will be more attuned to

the care needs of pregnant females.

With three or more sows it is prudent to stagger their matings so you are not overrun with babies that you do not have the time to socialize once they reach weaning age. It also enables you to have a steady flow of youngsters to sell, rather than have a large number and then nothing. With large numbers you may be tempted to sell them at reduced prices because you have limited accommodation. This actually does nothing for your future market, other than to bring down prices! It is always wise to develop your market outlets steadily, and build your herd in direct relation to these.

Breeding Age:
Female hedgehogs may become sexually mature by eight weeks of age, though males of a similar age will **rarely** be able to successfully impregnate a female. It is very unwise to mate a female before she reaches full physical maturity, which will be when she is at least six months old. This is also a good time to test mate a boar to a proven sow; likewise mate a maiden sow to a proven boar.

Breeding Condition:
Only breed hedgehogs that are in very good health. They should never be overweight, especially

Female hedgehogs are able to start a family when they are only eight weeks old! It is recommended that you wait until both male and female are six months old before you allow them to reproduce.

The time lapse between fertilization and birth is a little more than one month. Matings are over in a few minutes but may be repeated often.

the sow, as this could result in birthing problems. It is wise to deworm the female just prior to her being mated.

Mating:

It is normal for the sow to be taken to the boar's home and be left with him for two to four days according to his owner's policy. Fees should be agreed ahead of time and committed to a contract. Your contract should state whether or not a repeat mating will be given free in the event of non-pregnancy. As there can be complications over identification of hedgehogs, you should not count on repeat matings unless you are on very friendly terms with the boar's owner.

The hedgehog is an induced ovulator, meaning she comes into breeding condition, initially, with the presence of a boar, and specifically sheds her eggs as a result of stimulation by his penis. The estrus period in hedgehogs does not appear to be known for sure, but it is thought to be of very short duration. This means until she is actually pregnant she is always ready to be bred within any cycle of a few days.

After an initial, sometimes hectic, courtship, the female will allow the male to mount her. She lays her spines flat to her body and the mating is over within a few minutes, but is repeated a number of times. Between matings the pair may stay close to each other, or remain apart.

Gestation Period:

This is the time lapse between the fertilization of the eggs and the actual birth of the offspring. Within the genus *Atelerix* it is 35 days, give or take a few days. It is best to work on the basis of 35 days and mark your calendar or record cards accordingly from the day the sow was placed with the boar.

Litter Size and State:

The litter range in hedgehogs is 1-10 with 4-6 being typical. The young are born white; the tiny spines are covered with a membrane that shrivels away within hours of their birth.

CARE OF MOTHER AND OFFSPRING

About 5-7 days prior to the anticipated births, give the housing a thorough cleaning. By this time, the sow's food intake will have steadily increased and will continue to do so until it is time to start weaning the hoglets. Once the final pre-birth house clean has been done, do not disturb the female again until the babies are 2-3 weeks of age, unless circumstances dictate this as being critical. What is meant by this is that you must remove fecal matter and, of course, supply food, but do not handle the sow; remove dirtied floor material with a spoon. When the babies are born you may be very tempted to handle them. This could be fatal for the youngsters. Hedgehogs are very sensitive creatures and the slightest upset can result in the mother abandoning her babies—but more likely killing them as a protective urge. She may do this in any case if it is her first litter. At such a time females can become frightened and confused. She may scatter the litter around the accommodation and be at a loss of what to do.

If this is the case give her about 30 minutes to collect the babies. After this time you must gamble and intervene. Using a sterile spoon, gently lift the babies and place them into the nest box, or in the crude nest the female may have preferred to prepare outside the nest box. With luck she may calm down and thereafter care for her litter.

If the first litter is cannibalized, future litters may not be. If they are, this either indicates a poor mother who should not be used for further breeding, or a problem in the environment which is upsetting the sow. She may also be unfit and undernourished. You must establish which is the case. The fact that other sows are having litters without problem does not mean that environmental conditions are not bothering the cannibalistic mom.

Assuming that all goes well you will need to supply much larger than normal quantities of food because the babies grow at a rapid rate, and mom needs to keep the milk supply up. If in the first week or two the babies wander out of the nest box, they should be replaced using a large plastic spoon. Avoid touching them until they are at least 3-4 weeks old in order to reduce the risk that the mother might abandon or mutilate them. Only as you get to know the nature of the mother is it worth risking handling them at an earlier age. Once you have such a female you may be able to handle the babies within their first week of life. This will be very beneficial in the bonding process and makes them really fine little pets.

The youngsters are weaned from their mother's milk at any time after 3-4 weeks of age. By this time they will have been sampling solid foods for 1-2 weeks. The weaning process can take 2-3 weeks to complete. With a large litter it will take longer. Never be in a rush to sell your youngsters. It is important that they really are independent of their mother and eating well on their own before you give them up. At 6 weeks of age

Hedgehogs can have up to 10 babies at one time, but 5 is a good average.

is when you can begin to put in many hours handling them. You should also allow them to become familiar with the sort of everyday noises and day-to-day comings and goings that will be typical in their future home.

SELECTING STOCK AND SELLING

Making selections from litters for retention is never easy. Often, all the babies look nice so it is a case of being able to pick out those that display better color, are of the required size, have sound conformation and, most important, appear to be more tractable than others in the litter. The more litters you breed, the better your judgment will become. You will have more experience, and have the benefit of your breeding records to help you.

You should not assume that there will always be a youngster worthy of retention for future breeding. Sometimes there will be no obvious babies of merit—another time you may keep two or more from a litter. Bear in mind that youngsters do change as they mature, so a good looking baby may not be so outstanding when it is six months old. If it was retained because it showed promise that it does not

Hedgehog babies often roll up into a ball with their spines extended to protect themselves from being eaten.

achieve, sell it. The marketing of your youngsters should commence as soon as your sow is mated, or even earlier. Your selling options are basically of two sorts. One is direct to the public, the other is to pet shops. If you try to sell direct to the public you'll be letting yourself in for a bundle of headaches you might not be prepared to deal with. Additionally, if you sell direct to the public most pet shops won't want to deal with you, because you'll be in direct competition with them. Of course, when you sell to pet shops the stock must be discounted so the shop can retail them at much the same price that you would sell to the public. You will therefore make less profit

per hedgehog, but you will probably sell more at a time, and will have the benefit of repeat business. But keep in mind that many pet shops routinely shy away from buying stock from their customers, for a number of very good reasons—not the least of which is that if they buy from one customer they can develop friction with other customers who also might want to sell their excess stock.

BREEDING RECORDS & IDENTIFICATION

   Each boar and sow should have their own record card, and there should be a breeding log as well. On the individual's card you should record their number, sex, age, color pattern, size and

weight (taken at earliest age, 6 and 12 months). Give a grading number to their temperament once they are adult. Good mothers, and those that prove useful as fosters, should be noted. Bear in mind that a poor mother may have inherited this trait via her father, so do not always assume it must have come from her mother.

   This card can also note the number of times the hedgehog has been mated, to whom, and the results (number of offspring). Finally, it should note any illnesses, so that it is a complete life history of that hedgehog. It is useful to have a photo of each hedgehog clipped to their record card, or a drawing of their color pattern if this is unusual.

   The breeding log will record all details of each mating. This will be the number and names of parents, their colors, and the date of the mating. It will indicate date of births, gestation period, number in litter, and number that survive to selling age. Any abnormal babies will be noted. Record the colors of the offspring, their size and weights (as soon as this can be done), and of course their sexes.

   It would be beneficial, especially if your herd is growing, to keep a separate medical log. This will record all illnesses, treatments,

Hedgehogs look alike. In order to have a successful breeding program you must be able identify your hedgehogs and this is best done by keeping them caged and numbering the cages.

You can mark the belly of the hedgehog with a marking pen or you can use an ear tag. Ear tagging is more professional but it hardly is a humanitarian thing to do.

and results. The more detailed your records, the better able you are to trace problems, and to ponder the merits of given matings before they are effected. With regard to individual identification of your stock, the simplest means is by using a non-lead water soluble paint. By marking given areas of your hedgehog's body with a given color, you can devise a system to cover both sexes, and each breeding animal. Ear tagging is more permanent, and microchip implants may well become the standard form for permanent identification.

HEDGEHOG HEALTH CARE

Hedgehogs are very hardy little mammals, and unless you are either unfortunate, or lacking in general husbandry techniques, it is unlikely that you will experience anything other than minor problems. At this time the average veterinarian has little practical knowledge of treating these pets, which means that preventative husbandry is very much the order of the day. There are no specific vaccines developed for hedgehogs, so there is an element of pioneering and trial and error in the event a pet should contract a major illness. For these reasons breeders, in particular, should keep detailed records of problems and treatments. These can be passed to the NAHA for dispersal to other breeders.

GENERAL HYGIENE & CARE

Very often, illness in a pet is a direct result of the owner not ensuring that hygiene and care levels are satisfactory. This results in general debilitation. In turn this allows pathogens (disease causing organisms) to multiply to the degree that they totally overwhelm the animal's immune system; a major illness is the consequence.

Your pet's housing must be thoroughly cleaned at least once each week. Often, in small cages, this should be done twice per week. Food dishes should be washed every day before each meal is given. Automatic water dispensers should be cleaned daily, and kept filled so there is always water available. Your pet can drink quite a lot of water during the warmer periods, so do check the bottle each day. The breeding female will consume much more than normal. Never leave soiled floor covering in the vicinity of the cage(s): throw it away at each cleaning.

An underfed hedgehog is an unhealthy hedgehog so be very sure that your pet is receiving adequate quantities of food, and of the needed quality. All foods should be fresh and stored in cool, dark cupboards, or the refrigerator, depending on their type.

Handle your pet on a regular basis. This will enable you to give it a physical examination easily when needed. Every time you handle your hedgehog you should look for any cuts or abrasions, any parasites in the fur, any signs of swelling, and any indication of diarrhea in the form of staining to the anal area fur. Hedgehogs often lose a claw due to their scratching habits against cage doors. This can indicate they are stressed, so do be sure your pet is getting adequate time out of its cage.

Other signs of illness will be weeping eyes, runny nose, noisy breathing, and vomiting. Behavioral indicators would be disinterest in food, excessive scratching, prolonged drowsiness, and disinterest in what is going on around them when they would normally be awake and on the move. If they were normally happy to be picked up but suddenly indicate shyness, this may

" Do not attempt to diagnose and treat your own pet. This could prove to be fatal. "

be because it is causing them pain. If any of these situations persist, you should not delay in contacting your vet. If the problem can be diagnosed before it reaches an advanced stage it will be easier (and less costly) to treat. Do not attempt to diagnose and treat your own pet. This could prove fatal. You may make an incorrect diagnosis and supply an inappropriate medicine. Often, your vet will need blood and fecal samples so that microscopy can be used to identify causal agents. Until this is done it is not possible to administer a suitable drug or treatment.

WHAT YOU SHOULD DO

If you suspect that your pet is ill there are two things you should do that may help it and your vet.

1. Make notes of the reasons you suspect an illness—physical and/or behavioral indicators. Note the temperature in the area of your pet's housing. It is useful if you know the normal and present weight of your pet.

2. Isolate the hedgehog from other pets, and its own kind if two or more are kept. Be sure the pet is in a warm, not drafty, location.

Now phone the vet for advice.

If you have not followed the advice given, and have allowed a few days to elapse before contacting your vet, try to make some notes before doing so. The

following information may prove useful to the vet.

1. When did you first suspect an illness, and what prompted this? Have other clinical or behavioral signs become apparent, in what order, and against what sort of time lapse?

2. Note diet items in recent weeks.

3. How long have you

Finding a suitable technique for injecting a hedgehog requires experience. These three photos show you successful methods of injecting with one or two people participating.

owned the hedgehog, and what was its source—pet shop, breeder, friend, or wherever?

4. Has your pet, or other pets in your household, been ill recently, and what was diagnosed?

5. What actions have you taken so far, if any?

As a matter of record the normal rectal temperature of

the hedgehog is in the range of 93-98.6°F (34-36.7°C). During hibernation or estivation the temperature will drop dramatically. This fact should be remembered if the conditions your pet is living under are cold—it may not be ill, but simply cold enough to have gone into a torpid condition.

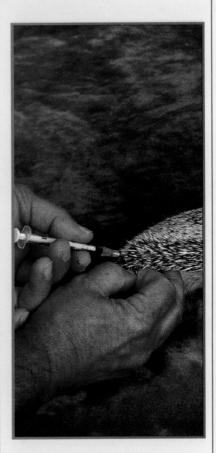

THE HOSPITAL CAGE

It may be that you live in a rather remote area and are unable to readily travel to a vet. If this is so, it would be wise to own your own hospital cage. This would also be a useful unit to have if you are a breeder. You can purchase commercial units, but often their cost is prohibitive for the average person, who can devise a very successful unit at a relatively modest price. You will want an infrared lamp wired to a thermostat, one or two thermometers, a wooden or plastic crate (or a parakeet stock cage), a nest box with numerous holes drilled in the top and upper sides (to allow good air flow), and food and water receptacles. If you purchase a stock cage, or other wooden unit, this should be well-coated with a non lead washable paint. If the unit is enclosed on all four sides, it should be fitted with a weld wire top to prevent the hedgehog from escaping, unless the side walls are a minimum of 30cm (15in) high.

Place the infrared lamp towards one end so your pet can move away from the heat source if it so wishes. One of the thermometers should be at one end, near the heat source, the other at the opposite end. This would only apply if the hospital unit was of greater length than width. If only one thermometer is used, place this as far from the heat source as possible so you can control the minimum heat level. The lamp may be clamped to cage fronts using special clamps that can be purchased with it, or it can be suspended above an open (or weld wired) topped unit. Be sure there is no risk that your pet could burn itself on the lamp, or on the weld wire top, or cage front.

The desired temperature setting should be about 90°F(32°C). Two or three degrees higher may not be amiss, but it increases the possibility that the patient might suffer from heat stress. This could be counter-productive to your objective. If you do not have an infrared lamp you can alternatively use a regular

Pet shops have many different types of exercise wheels. Always have one available for your pet hedgehog so they can get some exercise.

household light bulb of about 75 watts (you will need to experiment with this item to establish which will create the needed temperature relative to the size of the hospital unit). The drawback to household bulbs is that you do not have controlled heat, and you have high light intensity, which is not required. However, they are better than nothing in an emergency.

If you have occasion to use your hospital unit do be very sure to acclimatize the patient back to its normal living temperature once it has recovered. This should be done 2-3 degrees per day and never rushed. This could prompt a relapse and a chill. The unit must be thoroughly disinfected after each use.

QUARANTINE
If you own a hedgehog and acquire an additional specimen, and most certainly if you are a breeder with a steady flow of additional stock, quarantine of newly acquired individuals is strongly advised. The quarantine period should be a minimum of 14 days regardless of how good the source of the added stock was. During this period any incubating problems should manifest themselves. The quarantine area should be a cage as far away from your other stock as possible— meaning in another room or building.

At the same time you have the opportunity to routinely deworm and treat for external parasites should this be deemed necessary. For a worm egg count, your vet will need a fresh specimen of your hedgehog's fecal matter. Also during the quarantine period you can monitor the new addition's feeding habits, and acclimatize it to the temperature at which your own stock is maintained. Be sure to ask the seller what temperature they maintain in their hedgehog's housing, and what their feeding regimen was. The smoother the transition from one home to another, the less risk there will be of stress-related problems.

TREATING MINOR PROBLEMS

Problems that might be described as minor would include chills, external and internal parasites, and minor cuts and abrasions. It should be added that it is quite possible, from a minor condition, that secondary infections could result in major diseases, so never assume the term "minor" implies unimportant. Bacteria can gain entry to the blood system via a small cut, while a chill could result in a major respiratory problem if it is not quickly attended to.

If your pet displays weeping eyes, or a rather runny nose, you should transfer it immediately to a draft free and warm location. If the condition persists after 24 hours consult your vet—it may be more than a chill. External parasites, such as lice, fleas and ticks, are easily eradicated using modern treatments from your vet. Be sure to dispose of all bedding and floor covering material, clean the accommodation with bleach, then rinse with water. Finally, treat the accommodation as well. Repeat treatments may be required to kill eggs that hatch after the initial treatment—which may not be lethal to such eggs.

Internal parasites require species specific drugs, so your vet must effect a fecal examination to identify which are present in the sort of numbers regarded as being dangerous. Never treat for worms unless you know your pet has them, and what sort they are.

Minor cuts and abrasions should be gently wiped clean using tepid water, then a suitable antiseptic ointment or liquid applied. This will keep the site bacteria free while it heals, which should only take a few days. Any bald areas on the skin, or the loss of numerous spines, suggests a more serious condition, possibly fungal, and should be referred immediately to your vet.

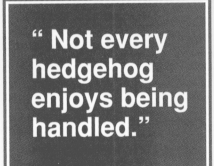

" Not every hedgehog enjoys being handled."

STRESS

A major precursor of illness in many pets, and quite possibly very much so in a pet like a hedgehog, is stress. The greatest problem in dealing with this condition is identifying it. This is because the situations that create it do not affect each animal in the same way. It is generally agreed that stress is most likely when the conditions an animal is living under are far removed from what is natural for that animal. There are other stressors that have been identified in most pets, and the conditions that will likely create them can be summarized as follows.

1. **Moving home.** This is a prime stressor, so make this as unchanging as possible in respect to food, hours of daylight, temperature, and general intrusion routine.

2. **Cramped living conditions.** If a pet does not have a reasonable space in which to exercise, or the opportunity to do so on a regular basis outside of its housing, it will likely become stressed.

3. **Dirty living conditions.** No animal likes to live in unclean conditions. These are totally unnatural for any animal. When forced to stay in such conditions the only result can be stress and problems.

4. **Excessive handling.** While you should handle your pet as often as possible this does not mean it

should be disturbed when it is asleep. Also, it must not be assumed that every hedgehog enjoys being handled to the same degree. Only careful observation can give you clues on this latter point. Mishandling by children or adults will stress a pet.

5. **Fluctuating temperatures.** It is wholly unnatural for a hedgehog to be subjected to rapid changes in its living environment. Try to maintain this as constant as possible, with changes taking place only over days or weeks, not hours.

6. **Intensive light.** Hedgehogs are creatures of the night. While they do adjust to daytime activity they should never be subjected to intense lighting. Keep it subdued.

7. **Excessive noise.** Hedgehogs have acute hearing, so should not be subjected to loud noises when they are sleeping.

8. **Inadequate diet.** Provide enough nutritious food daily.

EFFECTS OF STRESS
Stress may show itself in a number of ways. These are noted below but must be qualified with the comment that in all instances there could be an alternative reason for the actions stated. However, if obvious alternatives are discounted this leaves you with stress

as a very possible cause of a given problem.

1. **Aggression.** This is an obvious effect.

2. **Pacing or weaving.** Animals that are stressed will develop a compensatory action to try and relieve their tension. Pacing at the exit of their accommodation is very commonly seen, and is quite unnatural for any animal.

Find a veterinarian in your local area that is capable of caring for a hedgehog pet.

3. **Coprophagia.** This means eating fecal matter. It is often the result of dirty accommodation and incorrect diet, or a missing item in the diet. Other syndromes are wood, and hair eating (ligno- and trichophagia).

4. **Clawing.** A stressed hedgehog may claw at the cage door or at the cage floor. It is a tension

releasing activity usually caused by lack of space.

5. **Self-mutilation.** This is a variation on trichophagia, but the animal bites at its legs, tail, or other part until blood is drawn. Chronic lack of exercise is often the problem.

6. **Cannibalism.** A stressed female may kill and eat her own offspring. The stress may be the result of one or more of the stressors discussed. Sometimes a very well-established stress behavior can be difficult to cure, such as fecal or hair eating. They become strongly reinforced by the very action itself. But usually, stress behaviors subside and disappear when the underlying reason for them is corrected.

VETERINARY CHECKS
The final way in which you can minimize the risk of your pet ever becoming ill to any degree is by taking it for a veterinary examination on a regular basis. This should be done about every three months. During such visits you will gain much worthwhile practical knowledge just from general talks with your vet as he or she inspects your hedgehog. It is, of course, very important that your pet is friendly otherwise it will simply roll up into a ball of spines—making examination a prickly business!

HEDGEHOG SPECIES

Depending on the classification that is being followed, there are about 14 species, and a variable number of subspecies, of hedgehogs. Additionally, there are a further four species of hedgehog-like insectivores known as tenrecs. These are found in Malagasy (formerly Madagascar) and not available to the average hedgehog hobbyist.

The hedgehogs that have created this new hobby are from the genus *Atelerix*, though certain of its members are placed into the genus *Erinaceus* by some authorities. In broad terms, all hedgehogs are rather similar in appearance and color, so identifying species is not easy. Often, it comes down to inspection of skeletons in order to establish aspects of dental arrangements, skull lengths and other features.

Matters are not made any easier for the hobbyist with the lack of literary works devoted to hedgehogs. These are confined to scientific papers, plus chapters on the species in general zoological works. The following is therefore a brief synopsis of salient facts presently available on this group of fascinating little mammals. For reasons of space it is restricted to discussion of the genera with some species notes. The name following the genus is that of its author, and the date of first publication.

GENUS *ERINACEUS* LINNAEUS, 1758

Three species are recognized. *E.europaeus* (European hedgehog), *E.concolor* (Eurasian hedgehog) and *E.amurensis* (Amur hedgehog). The range of distribution is from Britain and Mainland Europe, through Asia Minor to Siberia, and south to China. Size ranges from 13-30cm (5-12in) and weight 400-1100g (14-39oz). The tail is short (1-5cm) and sparsely covered with hair. The normal color of the non-barbed spines is yellowish at the tip, then brown, then

The European hedgehog.

brown or cream at the base. The overlapping spines present a pattern known as agouti.

The facial mask and undercoat are brownish through light gray. However, the natural range of colors is considerable. Some individuals may appear very dark brown, others almost white. This applies to both the spines and the soft fur of the face, legs, and underbelly. A mask is normal, though it may range from very light to almost black. Color is not a reliable guide in distinguishing *Erinaceus* from other genera.

The hallux (first digit of the hind leg) is well developed. This can serve as a point of identification from *Atelerix*, where it is often absent, or much reduced if present. There are normally five pairs of mammae but, like color, the number of teats is not a reliable guide to distinguishing between hedgehog genera. The number of teeth is 36, but this is variable, and may be more. Gestation period is 31-35 days and the litter range is 1-7.

Members of the genus have been kept and raised as pets for centuries in Europe without ever gaining great popularity. They are very familiar mammals to most Europeans and are normally encouraged to stay within the garden area. In Britain they are a protected species and it is illegal to breed and sell them.

GENUS *ATELERIX* POMEL, 1848

There are four species in this genus. *A.albiventris* (White-bellied hedgehog), *A.sclateri* (Sclater's hedgehog), *A.frontalis* (South African hedgehog), and *A.algirus* (Algerian hedgehog). The distribution range is from southern Europe to South Africa, and from Senegal to northern Somalia, thus covering most of Africa. Size ranges from 17-23cm (7-9in) making them intermediate between the largest and smallest

The White-bellied hedgehog from Africa is the most common one used as a pet animal in the USA.

members of *Erinaceus*. Weight is in the range of 250-750g (9-26oz), so they are lighter than the average Eurasian hedgehogs. The tail is sparsely haired and of the same length as in *Erinaceus*. The reduced or absent hallux distinguishes them from the other hedgehog genera.

The color range is comparable with Erinaceus, though the underbelly of *A.albiventris* is normally very light, often white. The number of mammae is recorded as being three pairs but four or five pairs are typical for most members now in captivity. *A.albiventris* is the smallest member of the genus. It is entirely possible that domestic stocks may be hybrids of at least two or more species, though most are sold as being *albiventris*—if indeed the scientific name is used at all. The typical gestation period is 35 days, and the litter range is 1-10, thus somewhat larger than in *Erinaceus*. *A.frontalis* is listed as a threatened species. It is regarded as being rare in its native homelands due to human pressures of keeping it as a pet, as a food item, and to habitat destruction.

GENUS *PARAECHINUS* TROUESSART, 1879

There are three species in the genus. *P.aethiopicus* (Ethiopian or North African desert hedgehog), *P.hypomelas* (Brandt's

desert hedgehog), and *P.micropus* (Asiatic or Indian desert hedgehog). The range of distribution is from Mauritania and Morocco, east across northern Africa to Arabia, Iran, Pakistan, and India. The size range is 14-28cm (5.5-11in) making certain of its members the smallest of the hedgehogs. Weight is in the range of 300-500g (10-18oz). The tail is comparable to that in other genera.

The spines of some members may be rugose (wrinkled surface) and this may help to identify them from other genera. Coloration follows that typical for other genera, except that there is a greater tendency towards dark or light colors. The banding may be brown and yellow, black and white, or black and yellow. The number of mammae is four or five pairs. The gestation period is circa 35 days; the litter range 1-6.

It is quite possible that a number of the hedgehogs now popular as pets are of this genus. There is a need for a more detailed study of pets in order to establish which species they are, and to try and keep the species pure.

GENUS *HEMIECHINUS* FITZINGER, 1866

Four species are recognized. *H.auritus* (Long-eared desert hedgehog), *H.collaris* (Indian Long-eared desert hedgehog), *H.dauuricus* (Gobi Long-eared desert hedgehog), and *H.hughi* (Hugh's or Shaanxi Long-eared desert hedgehog). The distribution range is the Ukraine to Mongolia, Libya to northern India, and the Gobi desert and parts of central China. It is also found on the island of Cyprus in the Mediterranean Sea.

Size in the genus is within the range of 15-28cm (6-11in), while the weight range is comparable to *Atelerix*, 340g (12oz) being a typical mean average. Tail is as for other genera. The color pattern is white tipping, then brown and white banding. The underparts are gray-white, but the natural variation curve probably goes from very light to very dark as in other genera.

An obvious feature of identification in this genus is the long ears. These are erect and thought to be adaptations for the dissipation of heat in their desert homelands. Another mark of identification is that these species lack a spineless tract on the crown of the head. In *Erinaceus* this is narrow, in *Atelerix* somewhat broader, and at its widest in *Paraechinus*.

The gestation period is 35-42 days, thus longer than in the other genera. The litter size is 2-6 depending on the range: it is smaller in the eastern part than in the mountainous west.

It is reported that the long-eared hedgehogs are more aggressive than the species of other genera. But the sampling may have been small and therefore not a reliable guide to temperament. They would make a welcome addition to the hobby if it can be established, as this author suspects, that they are in fact as tractable as other species.

> " . . . there are about 14 species, and a variable number of subspecies, of hedgehogs "

This is simply a White-bellied hedgehog color variety. It is NOT a different species because this color variety does not exist in nature.

Hedgehog Primer

SCIENTIFIC NAME:
Most popular species is *Atelerix albiventris,* (white-bellied hedgehog).

COLORS:
Spines banded in white and brown. May range from almost white to almost black. Underparts and fur white, but also variable.

SOCIAL STATUS:
Solitary once mature. Non breeding females may cohabit in large accommodation, but not recommended.

TEMPERATURE NEEDS:
Range 60-85°F (16-30°C).

LONGEVITY:
5-8 years

NUMBER DIGITS:
5 front, 4-5 rear.

NUMBER TEETH:
Typically 36

NUMBER MAMMAE:
3-5 pairs

BREEDING CYCLE:
Polyestrus. 3-4 litters per year

LITTER SIZE:
Range 1-10, 4-5 average

WEANING AGE:
4-6 weeks

AGE TO PURCHASE:
8 weeks or over

DIET:
Carnivorous. May take some fruit/plant matter. Typical diet cat food, worms & other invertebrates, cottage cheese, eggs, meat & poultry.

VACCINATIONS:
Not available at present time. Hygienic husbandry is the key to health care.

References

Grzimek, B. ed. 1975 Grzimek's Animal Life Encyclopedia, vol 10, Mammals, Von Nostrand Rheinhold, New York

Kelsey-Wood, D 1994 Hedgehogs, TFH Publications Inc, Neptune, NJ

Nowak, Ronald M. 1991 Walker's Mammals of the World, 5th ed, vol 1, Insectivora pp114-37, John Hopkins Univ.Press, Baltimore

Storer, Pat 1994 Hedgehogs, 3rd ed, Columbus, Texas

NAHA Hedgehog News, Various, North American Hedgehog Association, 601 Tijeras NW, Suite 201, Albuquerque, New Mexico 87102